fourth edition
redwood empire
wildflowers

Dorothy King Young at work.
Photo courtesy Peter Palmquist.

redwood empire wildflowers

Dorothy King Young

fourth edition

Library of Congress Cataloging in Publication Data
Young, Dorothy King.
    Redwood empire wildflowers.

    Published in 1964 and 1970 under title: Redwood empire wildflower jewels; and in 1976: Wildflowers of the redwood empire.
    Includes index.
    1. Wild flowers–California–Identification. 2. Wild flowers–Oregon–Identification. I. Title.
QK149.Y68   1976   582'.13'097941   76-12996

Books for a better world

Naturegraph Publishers, Inc.
3543 Indian Creek Road
Happy Camp, CA 96039
U.S.A.

Contents

This book is dedicated to the memory of Charles R. Young, whose helpful hand was always there. He took the exotic photo of Sugarsticks **Allotropa** virgata *on the cover, among others.*

Acknowledgments

Actually, our involvement probably all started when our local newspaper correspondent, Mrs. Olga Cossi, chose to picture and publicize some of Grandpa Charley's and my rare botanical finds. Or Jim McNamee and his good wife, Ruth, might be responsible, since they encouraged us to take some of those same rare specimens to the University of Washington Arboretum in Seattle. Or it could have been Blanche Wilson, who wanted us to go to that fine Wildflower Show in Boonville. Anyway we did manage to share some lovely, rare specimens of Heaths, Groundcones. Orchids and Wintergreens with arboretums, herbariums and botany departments all the way from Berkeley to Seattle.

It is fun to sit here trying to think up words strong enough to say "Thank you!" to the grand people whose pictures or inspirations have made our Dream Flower Book come true:

Alice and Merrel Ackley (photos 41 & 85), Dr. Dennis Anderson, Lula and Lloyd Barnes (photos 8, 13, 14, 31, 43, 62, 66, 68, 71, 79, 86), Dr. Paul Bowman (50, 52), Jerry Evans (7), Alice Felt (16, 30, 38, 48, 69, 80, 83), Carl Geldin-Meyers (82, 98, 101), Louise Hallberg (96, 111), Ruth Hass (92), Dora Hunt (74), Dave Imper (4, 27, 39, 110), E.F. and Lolabelle Jewett (6, 9, 21, 24, 32, 33, 54, 61, 104, 112, 114, 116), Eigel Jorgensen (117), Christine and Frank Kemp (3, 5, 10, 75, 77, 81, 97, 105), Walter Knight (28, 109), Bill Linton (70, 95), Roger MacFarlane (53), Dr. Gordon McBride (11), Donal and Mabel McCall, J. Ed McClellan, Hobart McDaniel (35, 67), Jim and Ruth McNamee, Roy Mitchell (15, 63, 113), Rolie O'Neal, Wayne and Martha Roderick (76), Frank Sappingfield and Family (119), Warren Totten (18, 94), Dr. Bob Werra (2), Ned Westover (78), Douglas Wemmer (40), Violet Wooden (72, 106), Charles Young (1, 12, 17, 19, 20, 25, 26, 34, 36, 44, 46, 49, 55, 56, 57, 59, 64, 84, 87, 88, 90, 93, 102, 115, 118, 120).

Special thanks for this revision go to Steven Darington; Dr. Doris Niles, U.C. Extension; John Thomas Howell, Curator of the Botany Department, California Academy of Sciences; Nezzie Wade, Humboldt State University; and Barbara and Vinson Brown of Naturegraph for their help.

Jewels of the Redwoods

Jewels! The very word brings to mind the glowing, shimmering beauty, the translucent loveliness of diamonds, rubies and pearls. Sugarsticks are, indeed, the jewels supreme of the Redwood Empire, but Ladyslippers, Calypsos, Groundcones, Phantom Orchids, False Pink Asparagus and the Pyrolas also have moments of indescribable elegance.

Eighty years of pleasant searching for wildflower beauties of the forest, the mountain meadows, and the seashore would fill, many times over, the pages presented here. Rather it is our hope that the lovely flower pictures, the general times when each may be found, and a few specific locations may whet your appetite for discoveries and written records of your own. "Finders-keepers" may be safely played with your camera.

If you have leanings toward building a natural wildflower garden in your yard be sure to plant your lilies, clintonia, ginger and redwood sorrel in a deer-proof enclosure. We secured permission from the owners to hike the nearby logging roads to look for plants already partly mangled and those in the path of immediate destruction. Several fine clintonia and lily specimens were planted on the trails and meadows of Grandpa Charley's Park, our own little mountain ranch near the lively coast town of Gualala, Mendocino County, California, where we lived from August 1961 until January 1974. Naturally we watched them almost daily to see if they would perk up. Some even were on the verge of blooming. Imagine our consternation upon returning from a trip to find the buds neatly clipped off as well as most of the leaves. Dusk brought the culprits into full view, a beautiful doe and her twin fawns.

Many of our wildflower jewels have already become relatively scarce and some may even be in danger of vanishing, so:

Don't trample or destroy; do treasure and enjoy !

A Few Suggested Wildflower Trips

Stretching from San Francisco into Oregon along California's picturesque coast, the Redwood Empire delights the visitor most when its attractions are wreathed in flowers. Dates and roads may change. Seasonal fluctuation merits checking your local media for blooming peaks.

Starting in March, flowering cherry trees bloom in the Japanese Tea Garden in San Francisco's 1000 acre Golden Gate Park, furnishing an appropriate beginning for the horticultural year. This event is followed by the San Francisco Spring Flower Show, at the Hall of Flowers—also in John McLaren's great park.

Then come blossom tours in Sonoma County such as the Prune Blossom Tour near Healdsburg through the Alexander and Dry Creek Valley areas; and the Apple Blossom Easter Tour around Sebastopol, with its miles of pink-and-white beauty. Thousands of motorists enjoy these tours each Spring.

The Rhododendron Festivals at Ft. Bragg and Eureka in April and early May, feature both wild blooms in their natural setting, and cultivated flowers on show along the residential streets and parks. The Garden Society of Marin and the Vintage Festival Committee at Sonoma both stage garden tours in May; and the Luther Burbank Rose Festival in mid-May commemorates the great naturalist's regard for his favorite flower.

Two notable flower exhibits are the Art and Garden Show at Guerneville in June, and the Marin Art and Garden Fair at Ross over the Fourth of July weekend. Another is the Smith River Easter Lily Festival—"Easter in July," held toward the middle of that month in the Del Norte community of Smith River, "Lily Capital of the West."

In August the communities of Fort Bragg and Eureka present Fushsia shows, while San Francisco's Hall of Flowers is decked with color for the City's annual flower show. Art In The Redwoods is also hosted at Gualala in August.

Worthwhile fall events are the Art and Garden Show at Guerneville in mid-September, and the Marin Garden Society's Fall Flower Festival at Ross toward the end of October. Throughout summer and fall the Redwood Empire's fine county fairs include magnificent floral displays for visitors to enjoy.

It's All Greek To Me!

... we're prone to say, with a shrug, when confronted with an unfamiliar term, and very often, in our scientific studies, we're SO right! It is Greek—or Latin. In attempting to understand the long and hard to pronounce botanical names I've tried to remember the meaning of the words from which they spring. For instance, our mariposas belong to the calochortus tribe or genus in the lily family. Since *Calochortus* means "beautiful grass" and mariposa is Spanish for "butterfly," because of the lovely markings within the silky blossoms, light soon dawns upon you, and the unusual names begin to make sense.

Can there be any doubt then as to the logic behind this particular naming technique? Indeed, the mariposas ARE beautiful. The Broomrape or Cancer-root family (Orobanchaceae), distasteful as these terms are, is more easily understood when one realizes that orobanche means "choke vetch." In the same helpful way *Ranunculus* means "little frog" and we all know that frogs and buttercups (of *Ranunculus* genus) are both found in damp places. *Mimulus* or "little mimic" just fits our monkey flowers. The word *wort* means a plant or herb, so that many family and plant names ending in wort become a bit more clear. Toothwort *(Dentaria californica)* indicates the tooth-like root growths on that particular plant, which has among the earliest of spring blossoms. The connection between the dentist and *Dentaria* is readily understood. In our prolific wild onion genus *Allium* means "garlic." Even the astonishingly long and forbidding looking scientific family names that nearly all end in ACEAE mean just that—plant family. In California we also have Spanish derivations. Manzanita denotes "little apple." Going a bit more deeply we find that the universally accepted generic name for our manzanitas is *Arctostaphylos*, or "food for bears." *Yerba* is Spanish for herb.

Did you ever hear that the common knotweed that spreads so tightly in our barnyard trails, and along heavily trodden paths everywhere, was called "White-Man's Footsteps" by the Indians? The more it was walked on, the better it grew, only flatter and knottier! What a responsibility we white people have in making sure our footsteps are worthy of the coming generations!

🐋 A lifetime ago I knew where to look for Indian Pipes. Where are they now? See photo no. 117, and look along the Chetco River, Oregon, and Smith River, California. 🐋

Classification of Flowers

This book is a popular introduction to wildflowers of the Redwood Empire and is not meant to be a technical reference to complete classification. More botanically complete books can be found at your local library. Nevertheless, this book can be used to classify all the plants described and pictured in its pages if careful use is made of both pictures and descriptions. To help you understand the names of flower parts, flower types, inflorescences (the way flowers are arranged on a plant) and the different types of leaves, the pictures on the next two pages will help you. Study these pictures carefully and learn the names so you will recognize and understand what the descriptions are talking about in the main part of the book.

The plant families in this book are not arranged in the way botanists usually organize them, but are placed in alphabetical order for ease of use by a beginner. In a sense this book can be thought of as a telephone directory to the more beautiful and interesting flowers of the Redwood Empire, with the family name being the prefix.

Unfortunately, botanists themselves are far from complete agreement as to the scientific arrangement of plant families. We like best Dr. Leroy Abrams magnificent four volumes on an *Illustrated Flora of the Pacific States,* which has the families arranged as follows:

Phylum PTERIDOPHYTA—Ferns.
Phylum SPERMATOPHYTA—Seed Plants.
    Class GYMNOSPERMAE—Cone-bearing Plants.
        Families: Taxaceae (Yews), Pinaceae (pines and firs),
        Taxodiaceae (Redwoods), etc.
    Class ANGIOSPERMAE—Flowering Plants.
        Sub-class MONOCOTYLEDONAE—Parallel-veined.
            Families: Typhaceae (Cattails), Sparganiaceae (Bur-
            reeds), Potamogetonaceae (Pondweeds), etc.
        Sub-class DICOTYLEDONAE—Net-veined Plants.
            Families: Sauraceae (Lizard's-tail Family), Salicaceae
            (Willows), etc., and ending with Compositae (Sun-
            flowers).

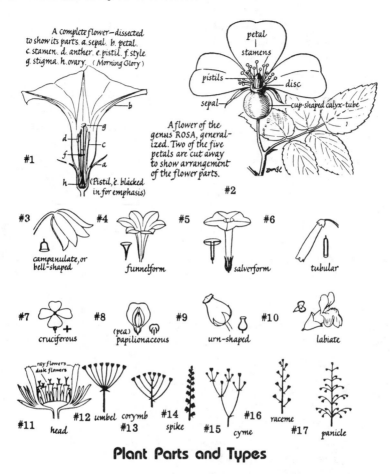

A complete flower–dissected to show its parts. a. sepal. b. petal. c. stamen. d. anther. e. pistil. f. style g. stigma. h. ovary. (Morning Glory)

#1

(Pistil, e. blacked in for emphasis)

petal | stamens
pistils
disc
sepal
cup-shaped calyx-tube

A flower of the genus ROSA, general-ized. Two of the five petals are cut away to show arrangement of the flower parts.

#2

#3 campanulate, or bell-shaped

#4 funnelform

#5 salverform

#6 tubular

#7 cruciferous

#8 (pea) papilionaceous

#9 urn-shaped

#10 labiate

ray flowers
disk flowers

#11 head

#12 umbel

corymb #13

#14 spike

#15 cyme

#16 raceme

#17 panicle

Plant Parts and Types

1 and 2. Two typical flowers, showing the names of their parts.

3 to 10. Types of flowers. 3 and 4 are *apetalous*, which means without distinct petals and sepals; 7 and 8 are *choripetalous*, which means the petals and sepals are each completely free from each other; 5, 6, 9 and 10 are *sympetalous*, which means the petals and sepals are all more or less closely joined together.

11 to 17. Types of flower formations. The daisy and sunflower look like single flowers, but really are heads of flowers (11).

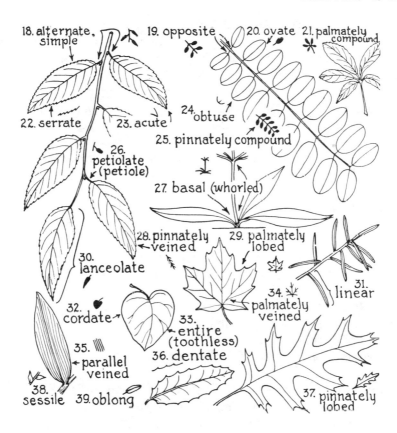

18. alternate, simple
19. opposite
20. ovate
21. palmately compound
22. serrate
23. acute
24. obtuse
25. pinnately compound
26. petiolate (petiole)
27. basal (whorled)
28. pinnately veined
29. palmately lobed
30. lanceolate
31. linear
32. cordate
33. entire (toothless)
34. palmately veined
35. parallel veined
36. dentate
37. pinnately lobed
38. sessile
39. oblong

18 to 39. Main types of simple and compound leaves. The small figure that is beside each big one shows the generalized shape from which every leaf form shown takes its name. Thus, *dentate* means toothlike and *serrate* means saw-like; *cordate* means heart-shaped and *linear* means like a line; *sessile* means the leaf has no stem or is stemless; while *petiolate* means the leaf has a short stem or petiole.

Note: The pictures shown on these two pages have been adapted from the book, *The Amateur Naturalist's Handbook,* by Vinson Brown, with the kind permission of the author and publishers, Simon & Schuster.

Habitats and Plant Communities

A habitat and a plant community may be considered synonymous in this book. Just as human beings form communities in their cities and towns, so plants form communities of associated plants. For the identification of the flowers as described and pictured in this book, a knowledge of the habitats in which each is found is often very important. You will notice that each plant described in this book has the habitats in which it is found listed. When looking for such a plant, watch for it in the correct habitats. The habitats and their abbreviations (if needed) appear below.

Beach—is a community of plants living along the ocean shore where they are subject to salt spray and winds and often have to dwell in sand. Also called **Sand** and **Sea Bluffs.**

Brush—is also called **Northern Coastal Scrub** and **Chaparral,** and is made up mainly of bushes, some with stiff branches, and many with small leaves to resist the heat.

Coniferous Forest (Conif.)—is the forest dominated by either the redwoods or the Douglas fir, with the forest floor carpeted thickly by the needles of these and similar trees.

Cultivated and Urban (Cultiv.)—includes farms, orchards, parks, towns, cities, etc.

Grassland (Grass)—is found in the lowland valleys and hills wherever grass is the predominant kind of plant.

Hardwood Forests (Hardwd.)—These forests are generally found nearer the coast than the oak forests, and often are found to take over temporarily land where coniferous forests have been burned. The predominant trees are tanbark oaks, madrone and bay or laurel trees.

Marsh—includes both fresh water marshes and swamps.

Meadow—Higher in the hills and mountains , grassy meadows are often found surrounded by coniferous forest.

Most Habitats (Most Hab.)—is a term used when a plant is found in many different habitats.

Oak Woodlands (Oak)—includes woods in which oak trees, such as the black and live oaks, are predominant.

Rocks—means rocky areas, cliffs, etc.

Savanna (Sav.)—is a grassland with scattered trees.

Streamside Woodland (Str. Wd.)—woods along streams.

Water—includes streams, rivers, ponds and lakes.

Conservation of Wildflowers

Conservation means "wise use." How can that simple statement be improved upon? When we apply the term to our natural resources we automatically think of our watersheds, minerals, forests, and streams. All, of course, are items of colossal importance. But now let us consider for a moment the conservation of beauty. How shall this be applied in our ultra-modern world? Shall we start with a fancy hairdo? We are such creatures of conformity that industry thrives as our demands surge upward to reach certain standards of conformity, even in regards to hairdos!

But I think it would be far more wonderful and significant if someone could only be smart enough to induce us all, as parents, grandparents, sisters, brothers, and friends, to strive to keep the stirring beauty of our great outdoors. We especially need to free it of the ugly roadside litter of cans, bottles and other debris of "civilization," and the destructive results of unwisely built roads or fly-by-night lumber operations, and the sick blotting out of beautiful landscapes by garish advertising signs. True enough, there are laws to cover the situation, and signs that plainly state that littering is illegal, yet the "strew-balls" go on with their selfish and fetid work without ceasing.

When sufficient interest is developed on our TV and radio and in our schools and clubs in the preservation of our natural beauties, perhaps the tide will turn. How we pray and hope and work that it will and trust you will join us! A number of interested naturalists, botanists, photographers, and plain wildflower-lovers, like Grandpa Charley and myself, have tried to point the way by carrying litterbags in our cars to help alleviate the disgraceful debris which so often mars our otherwise lovely scenery. We hope this book will give you a glimpse of the wonderful beauty we can all build if we seek to educate everybody to the need to preserve our wilderness.

How To Use This Book

Were it financially possible to produce a handbook of ALL our wild-flowers in full color that would retail at a reasonable price, we would do it. "One picture is worth a thousand words" is still as true as when the Chinese spoke it. Unfortunately, for many of the wildflowers described here words must suffice. Those for which we could not include a color photo are not referenced in the index but are interspersed throughout the text.

We have pictured nearly all of the still plentiful roadside beauties, a few really rare jewels, and have left space for you to record *your* findings. You should see the Young's field botany books! Margins are filled with notes of when, where, why, and whatever. Tacked on the wall of our favorite mountain house on Big Rock Ranch, Orleans, Humboldt County, we've kept long lists of botanical discoveries, year by year. In the interests of good housekeeping and on account of summertime spatters from cooking, these records have been destroyed. So keep your records in your own book so that you can compare them as the years go by. Imagine my own pleasure when I found a grandnephew's flower record tacked up alongside of mine!

Don't shy away from learning the scientific names. True, they are not easy, but they are accepted the world over. Sure, the eminent botanists *don't always agree*, but basically they are seeking to simplify our knowledge and make botany more complete and correct. Study the preceding pages carefully before you start using the picture section and learn the plant parts and forms, then study the habitats. When you start using the color plates and keys to identify the flowers you see, remember to study and compare everything most carefully, as it is easy to make mistakes since some flowers of different species are very similar.

The beautiful pictures that follow in the color plate section mostly show individual species of wildflowers, taken especially to aid in their identification as well as to give an appreciation of their beauty.

Keep looking and seeking. There is a lifetime of fun and joy in front of you if you really become a wildflower fan!

Color Plates and Identification Keys

1. Jewels of the forest. These beautiful forest jewels and rare flowers were gathered by Grandpa Charley and me from areas in the Redwood Empire that were being destroyed by loggers and others. Replanted, they were saved and then shared with herbariums up and down the coast where the exclamations of the viewers showed that many a professional botanist had never seen these rare gems together before. All of these, heaths, anemones, wallflowers, groundcones, coral root and phantom orchid, are mysterious children of the woods that we describe and picture later in more detail, but are here shown gathered in one glorious cluster.

2. Calypso (Redwood Orchids) and **Redwood Violets** spread a royal carpet, seemingly decked with fairy lanterns that beckon and twinkle in the filtered shade where, indeed, many miniature creatures of our woodlands might actually be holding forth. Near this forest sanctuary are aisles carefully laid out and marked with sword ferns, trilliums, and the brightly shining, heart-shaped leaves of wild ginger (5), which invite you to step gently and watch tenderly. Picture taken near Gualala, Mendocino County, which is also the home of Dorothy King Young Chapter of the California Native Plant Society and its renowned publication, the *Calypso* newsletter. Folks familiar with the general area here fondly refer to the overlapping habitats of Mendocino and Sonoma as Mendonoma.

✎ Arum Family—Araceae ~

3. Yellow Skunk Cabbage, *Lysichiton americanum,* usually grows under trees like alders, which are commonly associated with swamps, marshes and stream banks. Bruise one of the huge leaves to find out how it got its name. 1½ to 3 feet tall. Early Spring. Found in **Brush; Conif; Water; Marsh.** First found_____Where_____

Notes_____

_____

_____

_____

_____

The Redwood Empire forest.

1. Jewels of the forest

2. Calypso
Calypso bulbosa

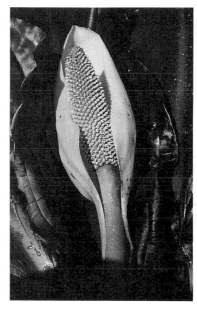

3. Yellow Skunk Cabbage
Lysichiton americanum

4. Oregon Grape
Berberis nervosa

ᴑ Barberry Family—Berberidaceae ᴑ

4. Oregon Grape, *Mahonia nervosa,* is found throughout the Redwood Empire. It has special significance in our Empire's northernmost fringe in Josephine County, Oregon, since it is closely related to Oregon's state flower, *Berberis aquifolium.* The glossy, green leaves with their spiny edges remind us of holly. 1 to 3 feet high. Found in **Conif.**
First found_____Where_____

ᴑ Birthwort Family—Aristolochiaceae ᴑ

5. Wild Ginger, *Asarum caudatum,* hugs the forest floor like a spicy rug near pools and seeps. The strangely shaped, dark red flowers have three long, tapering lobes; the heart-shaped leaves are shiny green above and red beneath. 3–4 inches high. Another variety (Hartweg's Ginger), has beautifully-shaped white-veined leaves; at higher altitudes. Found in **Conif.; Oak; Hardwd.**
First found_____Where_____

6. Dutchman's Pipe, *Aristolochia californica* (California Pipe Vine), is a twiner or climber with pendulous, greenish to purple, bowl-shaped flowers. 9–13 feet long. Found in **Str. Wd.**
First found_____Where_____

ᴑ Borage Family—Boraginaceae ᴑ

7. Hound's Tongue, *Cynoglossum grande,* is found in filtered shade, usually protected by scattered shrubs or trees. A large perennial (1 to 3 feet high) from a heavy root; the blooms are like big Forget-Me-Nots, exquisitely blue, borne in a loose cluster (panicle) at the top of the plant. Found in **Oak; Str. Wd.; Chap.**
First found_____Where_____

ᴑ Broomrape Family—Orobanchaceae ᴑ

8. Groundcone, *Boschniakia strobilacea,* is really a beautiful robber, since it is attached through a corm-like basal thickening to the root of its host, a madrone or manzanita. We have run across these strange parasitic growths the full length of the Redwood Empire clear north to Ashland, Oregon. Groundcone is exactly as pictured: thick, burgundy-brown as it

comes through the ground, each point developing into a soft beige, star-like blossom, which, as the summer progresses, turns into a fat, shining, ruby-red, translucent *jewel.* You will thrill anew at the wonders of earth when you find your first groundcone. 4–10 inches high; April–July. Found in **Most Hab.**
First found_____Where_____

9. Purple Ruffles, *Orobanche grayana* var. *violacea,* is still another beautiful robber. Apparently the seeds germinate and the rootlet attaches itself to the root of the host, the gum plant (*Grindelia*) as it grows on wet, sandy beaches. We have seen several specimens of this striking parasitic plant as they lay on the sand near the host after being kicked out of their snug resting place by the feet of children in Alder Creek State Park. 2–4 inches tall. Found in **Beach.**
First found_____Where_____

〜 Buckthorn Family—Rhamnaceae 〜

10. Whitethorn, *Ceanothus incanus,* is sometimes called white California Lilac, as the feathery plumes do resemble their cultivated "cousins" somewhat. The sharp, thorn-like branches try to catch you as you pass through the brush. The flowers are soft and branch freely in dense, compound panicles. This bush is often numerous and is one reason why chaparral is so hard to go through. 6–10 feet tall. Found in **Chap.; Str. Wd.**
First found_____Where_____

〜 Buckwheat Family—Polygonaceae 〜

11. Dune Buckwheat, *Eriogonum latifolium,* clings to the dunes and steep banks, always buffed by windy gusts from the sea. Perhaps the Greek interpretation of the word *Eriogonum*–woolly knees–has real significance for this particular buckwheat in its coastal form, as it is very hairy. The flowers appear in head-like clusters. 1–2 inches high. Found in **Beach.**
First found_____Where_____

Notes_____

5. Wild Ginger
Asarum caudatum

6. Dutchman's Pipe
Aristolochia californica

7. Houndstongue
Cynoglossum grande

8. Groundcones
Boschniakia strobilacea

False Pink Asparagus

Snowplant

🌿 Buttercup or Crowfoot Family—Ranunculaceae 🌿

Buttercups are probably one of the best known flowering plants in the world. Do you recognize these other members of the vast buttercup family?

12. Western Windflower, *Anemone deltoidea* (Western Wood Anemone), delights in lightly shaded spots in the mixed redwood forest. Each slender stem has three notched leaves about halfway up to the solitary, white flower that nods to you in the slightest breeze. 4–12 inches high. Found in **Oak; Conif.**
First found_____Where_____

13. Crimson Columbine, *Aquilegia formosa,* is a strikingly beautiful perennial frequently seen on road banks and woodsy edges of meadows. It has light green leaves that accent the nodding pale scarlet-petaled trumpets. The spurs contain much nectar for hummingbirds. The leaves form two sets of three leaflets. 1½–3½ feet high. Found in **Conif. Oak.**
First found_____Where_____

14. Blue Larkspur, *Delphinium decorum,* shows how well plants adapt to their environments. This stocky beauty is able to resist the coastal winds while similar relatives of the mountain swales and gullies are taller and more graceful. Leaves and stems covered with small hairs. 4–12 inches high. Found in **Grass; Brush.**
First found_____Where_____

15. Scarlet Larkspur, *Delphinium nudicaule,* is a flaming beauty. The oddly shaped bells or horns are daintier and more widely spaced than in the above flower, and the lower petal is cleft to about the middle. 8–32 inches high. Found in **Brush, Oak, Conif.**
First found_____Where_____

🌿 Dogwood Family—Cornaceae 🌿

16. Mountain Dogwood, *Cornus nuttallii,* often attains the height and stature of a tree, but the slender limbs, when clothed in their six inch, saucer-like blooms, look like a huge, well-arranged bouquet. Actually the blooms are the center cluster, but they are surrounded by the large, lustrous-white bracts, which appear to be petals. Sometimes called Pacific Dogwood. Twigs become dark red. 12–30 feet. Found in **Conif.; Str. Wd.**
First found_____Where_____

❦ Evening Primrose Family—Onagraceae ❦

17. Red Ribbons or **Lovely Clarkia,** *Clarkia concinna* (or Fringed Clarkia), likes to be neighborly on banks and bluffs where great colonies are seen splashing their rosy-pink cascades over the drying landscape. They glorify many a dry cliffside from June on. The flowers appear in the axils of the leaves; petals are clawlike. 1–2 feet. Found in **Conif.; Rocks.**
First found_____Where_____

18. Fireweed, *Epilobium angustifolium,* is known the world over as a rank, tall-growing perennial which springs from underground root-stocks. The panicles of densely hung, rosy flowers are beautiful until the cottony seeds begin to form; leaves net-like veined beneath. 1½–6 feet tall. Found in **Brush; Grass; Str. Wd.**
First found_____Where_____

19. California Fuchsia, *Zauschneria californica,* brings forth its glorious scarlet trumpets to relieve the monotony of our yellowing hillsides in late summer and early fall. Look for it clinging to the steepest, driest canyon walls. The base is usually slightly woody and the herbage is covered by very soft, tiny, green to gray spreading hairs; leaves linear to lanceolate. Plant 1–3 feet high. Found in **Rocks; Brush; Str. Wd.**
First found_____Where_____

20. Farewell-To-Spring, *Clarkia (Godetia) amoena,* will be seen in colonies of pink splashed with crimson on the drying roadsides and low hills. It is particularly brilliant on the very cliff edges above the ocean. 5–20 inches tall. Found in **Grass; Sea Bluffs.**
First found_____Where_____

❦ Figwort Family—Scrophulariaceae ❦

21. Chinese Houses, *Collinsia heterophylla,* may be seen sheltered under bushes that line road banks. The combination of colors in the flowers may differ, but all are pretty and the symmetrical flower whorls do appear something like the pagodas of China. In this species the upper lip of the corolla is distinctly paler than the lower lip. Very common in shaded places. 8–20 inches high. Found in **Brush; Grass; Oak; Str. Wd.; Sav.**
First found_____Where_____

9. Purple Ruffles
Orobanche grayana
var. *violacea*

10. Whitethorn
Ceanothus incanus

11. Dune Buckwheat
Eriogonum latifolium

12. Western Windflower
Anemone deltoidea

Calypso

22. Indian Warrior, *Pedicularis densiflora.* Sometimes out in the open, but more often in light shade, whole companies of Indian Warriors stand constantly at attention with their feet firmly planted in a cluster of fern-like, pale green or bronze leaves. In one of the pictures they are guarding newly opened Easter Lilies or Fawn Lilies or Lambstongues on a beautiful bank that is no more, as it was destroyed by a new road. Of course we do need safer mountain roads, but we need lovely wildflowers too! 4–16 inches tall. Found in **Oak; Brush; Conif.**
First found_____Where_____

23 & 24. Indian Paintbrush, *Castilleja wightii,* has yellow to reddish-orange flowers, with all hues in between. What appear to be splashy, colorful flowers, are really glorified bracts. This species grows as far north as the southern Mendocino coastal bluffs. At the north end of its range it has brighter red bracts and corollas and is called *C. wightii,* subspecies *rubra.* The common darker red paintbrush inhabiting the same bluff locations from about the Sea Ranch north is called the Mendocino Coast Indian Paintbrush, *C. mendocinensis* (or may be a subspecies of *C. latifolia),* and is not pictured here but looks superficially the same as *C. wightii* except for the rich red color. Several other inland paintbrushes are also found in our area. 8–15 inches tall. Found in **Sea Bluffs.**
First found_____Where_____

25. Scarlet Monkey Flower, *Mimulus cardinalis.* The glorious Scarlet Mimulus, as it is also called, is a vivid picture when seen in blossom against the clay or rocky banks where it is usually found, often with its feet in water. The soft, usually sticky foliage, is light green, the flowers crimson velvet. The pedicel or stem that holds the flower is longer than the calyx in this species and the stamens stick out above the corolla. 10–30 inches high. Found in **Str. Wd.; Oak; Grass; Sav.; Brush.**
First found_____Where_____

26. Purple Mouse-Ears, *Mimulus douglasii,* form masses of low-growing purplish flowers with prominent yellow anthers. The common name results from the flower having only two prominent corolla lobes. Plant is 1–3 inches tall. Kellogg's Monkey Flower, *M. kelloggii,* is on the left of the picture with all lobes fully developed and color rose-purple. Both are found in places which are damp in the spring. They are well distributed inland in rocky places. 1–8 inches tall. Found in **Rocks.**
First found_____Where_____

27. Yellow Monkey Flower, *Mimulus guttatus* (or Common Monkey Flower). A sharp look at the photo on page 38 easily explains the common name. The more tender varieties come out in early spring; watch for them in the wet places all summer. The corolla is usually spotted with red, and its throat almost enclosed with hairy ridges. 1½–36 inches. Found in **Str. Wd.; Grass; Water; Oak; Brush.**
First found_____Where_____

Orange Bush Monkey Flower, *Mimulus aurantiacus,* varies from orange to yellow in the flowers, and is common along the coast, flowering much of the year. 2–5 feet. Found in **Conif.; Rocks; Str. Wd.; Conif.; Oak; Brush.**
First found_____Where_____

28. Redwood Penstemon, *Penstemon corymbosus* (lately called *Keckiella corymbosa).* These plants like to show brick-red glory from roadside banks above and below your eye-level, so watch closely as you crisscross the inland Redwood Empire. Highway 101 north and south of Richardson Grove is a favorite finding place of ours. The plants seem to scramble over the steep roadside embankments. The stems are woody and the plants are up to 20 inches high. The upper corolla lip flares at a right angle while the lower lip spreads. It flowers profusely from August through October. The only common woody penstemon of this area. Found in **Rocks.**
First found_____Where_____

⚬ Four O'Clock Family—Nyctaginaceae ⚬

29. Yellow Sand Verbena, *Abronia latifolia.* The yellow flowers and very wide leaves of this plant, as it spreads in little mats on the beach, are quite distinctive. Like other sand verbenas, it has a quite deep and spreading root system to hold the plant when it is attacked by the fierce ocean winds. The prostrate stems are from 10 to 33 inches long and densely-hairy-glandular (sticky). Found in **Beach.**
First found_____Where_____

Notes_____

_____

_____

_____

_____

Leopard Lily

13. Columbine
Aquilegia formosa

15. Red Larkspur
Delphinium nudicaule

16. Mountain Dogwood
Cornus nuttallii

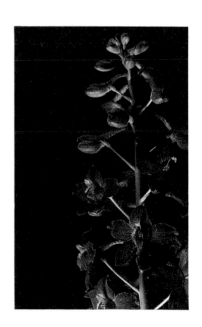

17. Red Ribbons
Clarkia concinna

14. Blue Larkspur
Delphinium decorum

30. Pink Sand Verbena or **Beach Sand Verbena,** *Abronia umbellata,* is pink most of the time, but sometimes white; the stems are often reddish and sometimes sticky to the touch; the leaves are more oval and not so wide as the above plant, and like most Abronias, rather fleshy in texture. The extraordinary ability of these beach verbenas to adapt both to shifting sand and a heavy salt content in the atmosphere and sand shows a most interesting specialization in living that these plants portray. 8–30 inch long stems. Found in **Beach.**
First found_____Where_____

✍ Fumitory Family—Fumariaceae ✍

31. Bleeding Heart, *Dicentra formosa,* ordinarily colonizes in damp, shady spots where the lovely pink to reddish hearts hang from the curving stem like bangles on a necklace. The cut-leaf, pale green, and fernlike foliage serves as a perfect foil for these precious woodland jewels. The leafless stems rise from a cluster of long, basal leaves to support the flowers in a compact panicle. 8–20 inches high. Found in **Conif.; Oak.**
First found_____Where_____

✍ Gentian Family—Gentianaceae ✍

32. Blue Gentian, *Gentiana oregana,* is rightly fabled in story and song. The deep blue of the sky and the pale blue of distant water in the early morning are caught in the gentian's bell or bottle-shaped blooms. Gentians are of different shapes, some tall and slender, others low-growing and sprawly, but always beautiful, with the showy flowers ranging from blue, through purple to white and even all yellow. There are just two common ones in our area, this Blue or Oregon Gentian, which has rather broad oval leaves, and the King's or Scepter Gentian *(Gentiana sceptrum),* which has narrower, lanceolate leaves. Both have blue flowers, but the *oregana* petals are green-dotted. 8–20 inches tall. Found in **Grass; Brush; Meadow.**
First found_____Where_____

✍ Heath Family—Ericaceae ✍

It would take several large books to do justice to the remarkable Heath Family. There is even confusion in the botanical world over the many different types of small flowering growths, bushes, and trees, all commonly known as heaths. Following the method of *A California Flora,* by Drs.

Philip A Munz and David D. Keck, we are placing our pyrolas, chimaphilas, sugarsticks, and a collection of unusually rare botanical specimens (often called heaths) in the Wintergreen Family at the end of this book.

33. Bearberry, *Arctostaphylos uva-ursi,* also called Kinnikinnick or sandberry, it is a low, prostrate shrub that throws up occasional erect branches, 2–6 inches tall. It has a darker-brown and less reddish bark than most of the manzanitas. The shining, leathery and oval leaves surround dense clusters of whitish or pinkish, urn-shaped flowers. Indians used the leaves for smoking and and a tonic in tea. Found in **Brush; Grass; Beach.**
First found_____Where_____

34. Common Manzanita, *Arctostaphylos manzanita,* also called Parry Manzanita. These erect shrubs are noted, along with related species, for their dark red and smooth (sometimes even glistening) bark. This species is noted for the combination of bright green leaves with hoary-white or grayish, hairy branchlets. The white or pink, urn-shaped flowers turn into first white, then dark red berries. 6–21 feet high. It is common on dry slopes, mainly in the interior. Found in **Brush; Oak; Conif.**
First found_____Where_____

35 & 36. California Huckleberry, *Vaccinium ovatum,* has shining, leathery green leaves with toothed edges and pale undersides; the white to pink, bell-shaped flowers are surrounded at first by red bracts, which fall off as the flowers turn into black edible berries. Often these many branched shrubs thickly cover the forest floor. This plant reminds us of Huckleberry pie and Huckleberry Finn, and other symbols of free wilderness life. 3–8 feet tall. Found in **Conif. Hardwd.; Brush.**
First found_____Where_____

Notes_____

_____

_____

_____

_____

18. Fireweed
Epilobium angustifolium

19. California Fuchsia
Zauschneria californica

20. Farewell-to-Spring
Clarkia amoena

21. Chinese Houses
Collinsia heterophylla

22. Indian Warriors
Pedicularis densiflora

23. Indian Paintbrush
Castilleja wightii

24. Indian Paintbrush
Castilleja wightii

25. Scarlet Monkey Flower
Mimulus cardinalis

26. Purple Mouse-Ears
Mimulus douglasii

37. California Rhododendron, Rhododendron macrophyllum, is also called California Rose-bay, and is one of our most stately and beautiful woodland shrubs. The dark green and leathery leaves are paler below; the spectacular, bell-shaped flowers are usually rose to rose-purple in color, rarely white, and appear in terminal umbels and racemes. 3–13 feet tall. Found in **Conif.; St. Wd.; Brush.**
First found_____Where_____

38. Western Azalea, Rhododendron occidentale, is a loosely-branched shrub with deciduous leaves and shredding bark. The leaves are much thinner and lighter green than in the California Rhododendron. The white to creamy or pink fragrant flowers are funnel-shaped and very beautiful, but not quite as spectacular as its relative; they appear in terminal clusters among the large, lance-shaped leaves; the upper lobe of each corolla often has a yellowish blotch. Probably no bushes in the forest, with the possible exception of the dogwood, attract so much attention in late spring as the azaleas and rhododendrons, whose large flowers often catch the few rays of sunlight like glowing cups and fill the woods with laughter and fragrance after winter dreariness. 3–15 feet tall. Found in **Conif.; Brush; Str. Wd.**
First found_____Where_____

39. Labrador Tea, Ledum glandulosum, has shiny, leathery leaves, finely-wrinkled above, and stiff, whitish-green twigs, often somewhat sticky to the touch, and giving off a fragrant odor; the white flowers appear in dense, terminal, umbel-shaped corymbs, starting as large and scaly buds. The flowers turn into round or oblong capsules. This plant is famous as a wilderness substitute for tea and is indeed believed delicious by many who drink it. 2–6 feet tall. Found in **Water; Marsh.**
First found_____Where_____

40. Salal, Gaultheria shallon, is usually a low and spreading shrub or sub-shrub, though sometimes tall and erect. The ovate or round leaves are sharp-pointed and finely-toothed, usually evergreen and are leathery to the touch. The white or pink, urn-shaped flowers appear in racemes and turn into dark purple berries with brown seeds. It is a typical shrub of damp woodlands. 1–2½ feet tall. Found in **Conif.; Str. Wd.; Brush.**
First found_____Where_____

Notes_____

~ Honeysuckle Family—Caprifoliaceae ~

Hairy Honeysuckle, Lonicera hispidula, with its opposite leaves, which are very closely set, climbs through bushes and trees, festooning them with dainty, sweet-smelling pink clusters during the summer. In fall and winter the flowers turn to sparkling rubies (fruits) that are not edible. The flowers form axillary whorls of spikes or loose panicles. 6–20 feet long or tall. Found in **Conif.; Oak; Hardwd.**
First found_____Where_____

41. Twinberry, Lonicera involucrata, is a non-twining shrub with its opposite leaves darker green above and paler and more hairy below. The flower stems usually turn reddish to purplish, each leading to two delicately perfect twin flowers, the pair held attractively in a cup-like set of bracts, and each corolla like a perfect little narrow bell. The twinberries or fruits are black and not edible. 2–10 feet. Found in **Str. Wd.; Oak; Conif.**
First found_____Where_____

~ Iris Family—Iridaceae ~

42. Wild Blue Iris, Iris douglasiana, also called Coast Blue Iris or Douglas Iris, is the most constant bloomer among our several kinds. Like many other Iris flowers, it seems to change color in a new locality. This species often sends out its first blossoms in late November. By February, in an open winter, the roads along the coast and the adjacent pastures are handsomely blue-dotted with them. This species has very long leaves, up to 36 inches long, dark green to yellowish-green and with reddish or pinkish bases; the large flowers vary in color from deep red-purple, through dark lavender and blue to pale cream. 10–20 inches tall. Found in **Grass; Str. Wd.; Oak; Conif.**
First found_____Where_____

Purdy's Iris, Iris purdyi, is another common local species of this genus. Also called Yellow Iris, it is smaller and has cream-yellow flowers, usually veined with purplish-brown or lavender and often lavender-tinged. Found in **Conif.; Oak; Hardwd.**
First found_____Where_____

Notes_____

27. Yellow Monkey Flower
Mimulus guttatus

28. Redwood Penstemon
Penstemon corymbosus

29. Yellow Sand Verbena
Abronia latifolia

30. Pink Sand Verbena
Abronia umbellata

31. Bleeding Heart
Dicentra formosa

33. Bearberry
Arctostaphylos uva-ursi

32. Blue Gentian
Gentiana oregana

34. Manzanita
Arctostaphylos manzanita

43. Blue-Eyed Grass or **Grass Iris,** *Sisyrinchium bellum.* This is the commonest of our Iris plants, filling many a meadow or grassland with its clusters of long, very slender and knife-like leaves from which the blue, violet, lilac or sometimes white flowers emerge in the springtime. The flowers turn into pale or dark brown capsules, filled with one to a few dark-pitted seeds. Its great numbers and ability to live in many different habitats show its wonderful adaptability to different environments. 4–20 inches tall. Found in **Grass; Brush; Str. Wd.; Oak; Conif.**
First found_____Where_____

Golden-Eyed Grass, *S. californicum;* has yellow flowers. Found in **as above.**
First found_____Where_____

☙ Lily Family—Liliaceae ☙

This enormous family has some of the most beautiful and unique flowers in all our area. First to be mentioned of these are the Wild Onions, of which about five species are found in the Redwood Empire. The three most commonly seen and wide-spread of these are mentioned below.

44. Magenta Wild Onion or **Coastal Wild Onion,** *Allium dichlamydeum,* frequents the edges of marshy areas in the open meadows. We have also found this bright magenta beauty growing in steep and rocky places. It looks for all the world like our cultivated amaryllis, or naked ladies, since the foliage is gone before the blossoms appear. The rank onion smell is most evident. The flowers form very congested umbels and their rich rose-purple color (magenta) is distinctive. Most wild onions are edible, at least at certain times of the year, but some are very bitter. 4–12 inches tall. Found in **Rock; Brush; Conif.; Grass.**
First found_____Where_____

45. Tall Brodiaea or **Blue Dicks** or **Wild Hyacinth,** *Brodiaea laxa,* is one of the several lovely Brodiaea species found in our valleys and hills. The blue or violet (rarely white) flowers are surrounded by purple bracts. The bulb is edible; leaves flat and keeled. 6–16 inches tall. Found in **Grass; Str. Wd.; Oak.**
First found_____Where_____

46. Dwarf Brodiaea, *Brodiaea coronaria macropoda* (or *terrestris*). This very low-growing form is particularly common in the meadows near woods. The

flowers are lilac to violet. Up to 3 inches tall. This is a dwarf form of the Harvest Brodiaea *(B. coronaria)*, which forms its flowers in a comparatively flat-topped umbel and is more common in the Great Valley, and is 4–15 inches tall. Found in **Conif.; Oak; Grass; Sand.**
First found_____Where_____

Blue Stars or Star-Flowered Brodiaea, Brodiaea stellaris. The perianth (sepals and petals) of this medium-sized Brodiaea flatten out rather abruptly in a way unusual in this genus to produce a star-like appearance, so that a number of them in a meadow appear very much like a group of scattered violet-purple stars with white centers. The bottoms of the perianth tubes are greenish. 4–12 inches tall. Found in **Grass; Meadow; Conif.**
First found_____Where_____

47. Chinese Firecrackers, Firecracker Flower, or Firecracker Lily, Brodiaea ida-maia, is, perhaps, our most distinctive native lily. It may be found dangling several bright red firecrackers, each scalloped with green, on grassy hillsides bordering mountain roads at elevations from 1000 to 4000 feet. It flowers in May to July. 1–3 feet tall. Found in **Grass; Meadow; Conif.**
First found_____Where_____

48. Redwood Lily, Lilium rubescens. This is the first of the magnificent tall lilies mentioned in this book, and, like the others, it has several common names (including Lilac Lily). Beauty is the attribute all have in common, and all grow in the Redwood Empire, but, like gold, they are where you find them! The 3–8 white flowers are purple-spotted, later turning wine-colored. Because it is the most common large lily found in the chaparral or brush, it is often called Chaparral Lily or even Chamise Lily, after the Chamise plant with which it is associated. 2–8 feet tall. A lovely flower of heavenly fragrance, it should be left alone. Found in **Brush; Conif.**
First found_____Where_____

Notes_____

_____

_____

_____

_____

_____

35. Huckleberry
Vaccinium ovatum

36. Huckleberry Fruit
Vaccinium ovatum

37. California Rhododendron
Rhododendron macrophyllum

39. Labrador Tea
Ledum glandulosum

38. Western Azalea
Rhododendron occidentale

40. Salal
Gaultheria shallon

43. Blue-Eyed Grass
Sisyrinchium bellum

41. Twinberry
Lonicera involucrata

42. Wild Blue Iris
Iris douglasiana

49. Tiger Lily, Leopard Lily or **Panther Lily,** Lilium pardalinum, has been called Tiger Lily so long that it is hard to take the name away from it, though Leopard Lily is a much more appropriate name because it is definitely spotted instead of striped. The flowers are rarely fragrant, as in the Redwood Lily, but, as they nod in the breeze (forming 1 to several on each plant), their orange (or red) color, spotted with maroon, makes them one of the most attractive sights in the woods. 3–7½ feet tall. Found in **Str. Wd.; Grass; Meadow; Rocks.**
First found_____Where_____

50. Kellogg's Lily, Lilium kelloggii, is found in dryer places than the Leopard Lily. Its fragrant flowers are large and distinctively pink or pale pink in color, with a central yellow band that is sometimes dotted with purple; the whole flower may turn rose-purple with aging; there are 1–15 or even more flowers on each plant, all with their outer edges rolled back. 2–10 feet tall. Found in **Conif.; Rocks.**
First found_____Where_____

51. Coast Lily, Lilium maritimum, strangely enough grows in masses on the edges of coastal openings and, at such places, appears actually in miniature. Normally it is 1–5 feet tall, with 1–12 horizontal and bell-shaped flowers, each dark red and spotted with maroon. It particularly likes raised hummocks in bogs, but also sandy soil. Botanists are constantly referring to the white plains of Mendocino, and The Pygmy Forest there is well-known for its tiny but full-grown plants, bushes, and trees. Nature plays us flower-lovers tricks sometimes, but it is a good teaching! Found in **Marsh; Sand; Oak; Brush.**
First found_____Where_____

52. Eureka Lily or Western Lily, Lilium occidentale, is particularly common near Eureka. It is found most often near the ocean and is distinguished by being usually dark red flowered or dark orange, with maroon spots; later it may fade to purple, but always has a green center in each flower. The flowers have the outer half recurving under. It likes wet places and is especially associated with ferns. 2–12 feet tall. Found in **Brush; Sand.**
First found_____Where_____

53. Bolander's Lily, Lilium bolanderi, is another very beautiful big lily with flowers varying from pale scarlet to deep crimson, each speckled with purple spots; only the upper margins of such flowers are rolled back; 1–4 inches tall. Found in **Brush; Conif.**

First found_____Where_____

54. Pitkin Lily, *Lilium pitkinense,* was formerly found only in the Pitkin Marsh, Sonoma Co., Calif. Now thought to be extinct in habitat, it is closely related to the Eureka Lily.

First found_____Where_____

55. Mission Bells, or **Checker Lily,** *Fritillaria lanceolata,* is extraordinarily varied in shape, color, and growth. Usually it is more somber in appearance than the big lilies just mentioned, but it's softer colors are often very spiritual and lovely in effect, particularly this species, whose delicate, hanging-bell-like flowers are mottled with yellow against purple-brown, or may vary to pale greenish-yellow, faintly mottled with purple, each appearing like a deep, upside-down bowl. Often found elf-like in shade. 1–4 feet tall. Found in **Brush; Conif.**

First found_____Where_____

56. Mendocino Mission Bells, *Fritillaria rodericki.* Found in scattered areas on the Mendocino coast and inland in Anderson Valley. Distinctive for the beige thumbnail delicately marked on each brown petal point. 8–10 inches tall. Found in **Sand; Grass.**

First found_____Where_____

57. Purdy's Fritillary, *Fritillaria purdyi,* looks something like Mission Bells, but has white flowers, mottled with purple lines and spots. 8–16 inches tall. Found in **Brush; Conif.**

First found_____Where_____

58. Scarlet Fritillary, *Fritillaria recurva* lives on dry hillsides in brush. The 1–9 nodding flowers are combined funnel and bell-shaped, bright scarlet, checkered with yellow within and tinged purple on the outside. There is a prominent oval, yellow gland with red spots. 1–3 feet tall. Found in **Brush; Conif.**

First found_____Where_____

59. Adobe Lily, *Fritillaria pluriflora,* is rather fantastic looking, with 1–3 nodding, bell-shaped, pink to pink-purple flowers, generally with brown veins outside. 8–20 inches tall. Found in **Oak.**

First found_____Where_____

44. Magenta Wild Onion
Allium dichlamydeum

47. Firecracker Flower
Brodiaea ida-maia

45. Blue Dicks
Brodiaea laxa

46. Dwarf Brodiaea
Brodiaea coronaria macropoda or *Brodiaea terrestris*

48. Redwood Lily
Lilium rubescens

49. Leopard Lily
Lilium pardalinum

50. Kellogg's Lily
Lilium kelloggii

51. Coast Lily
Lilium maritimum

53. Bolander's Lily
Lilium bolanderi

52. Eureka Lily
Lilium occidentale

The Mariposa Lilies of the Genus Calochortus are a particularly distinctive and beautiful group of flowers of our woods, each with delicate, fairy-like colors.

60. Hairy Cat's Ear, Hairy Star Tulip or **Pussy Ears,** *Calochortus tolmiei* (or *maweanus*), may be found in grassy meadows and along roadbanks. The ears may be grayish-lavender or yellow, but cat's ears they are, unmistakably. There is a very narrow, basal leaf, 4–16 inches long. The white or cream flowers are sometimes tinged with rose or purple, each petal having a beard on its inner face (as do most Mariposa Lilies). 4–16 inches tall. Found in **Conif.; Oak; Hardwd.**
First found_____Where_____

61. Baby Tulip or **Large-Flowered Star Tulip,** *Calochortus uniflorus,* looks very much like a baby tulip, but is noted also for its satiny flowers and the peculiar greenish-lilac sepals. The petals are generally lilac with a purple spot on each side of the gland, and much less hairy than the above flower. 4–10 inches tall. Found in **Grass; Meadow.**
First found_____Where_____

62. Diogenes Lantern or **Golden Fairy Lantern,** *Calochortus amabilis* (also called Yellow Globe-Tulip and Golden Fairybells), brightens our hilly roadsides with waxy, golden yellow lanterns set off by bluish-green foliage. The stout stems fork in pairs. 8–12 inches tall. Found in **Oak; Grass; Conif.**
First found_____Where_____

63. White Fairy Lantern, *Calochortus albus,* is similar looking to 62. The sepals are greenish-white, often touched with purple; the white petals are purplish at the base and with a patch of yellowish hair. 8–20 inches tall. Found in **Conif.; Oak; Hardwd.**
First found_____Where_____

64. Butterfly Mariposa Lily, *Calochortus venustus.* While the Spanish word Mariposa means butterfly, the Latin word *Calochortus* means beautiful grass. So the botanists chose very beautiful and appropriate names for the flowers of this genus. This flower is no more butterfly-like than any of the others, except that it may be called so because it shows so many different colors, with a brown spot surrounded by yellow on each sepal, while the petals are white or lilac with a prominent dark eye-spot in the middle and a

reddish blotch near the top. 4–32 inches tall. Found in **Grass; Meadow.**
First found_____Where_____

Yellow Mariposa Lily, *Calochortus luteus,* is noted for its wonderful deep yellow color, either streaked or spotted with brown on the petals. 6—20 inches tall. Found in **Grass; Meadow.**
First found_____Where_____

65. Slink Pod, *Scoliopus bigelovii,* also answers to the names of Fetid Adder's Tongue or Brownies. The names are suggestive indeed; the Greek derivation means "crooked foot" because of the twisted pedicels or stems. The mottled green and purple flowers have a bad odor. It is sometimes found as early as December 15 in the damp Mendocino County coastal area known as the "the Banana Belt." They literally spring from the ground in their haste to be the "first lily" to bloom. Dark mottled leaves are also distinctive 4–8 inches tall. Found in **Conif.**
First found_____Where_____

66. Cream Fawn Lily, *Erythronium californicum,* is also called Lambstongue, Easter Lily and Trout Lily, all on account of the spotted and mottled leaves. The usually reddish flower stems support 1 to 3 or more white to cream colored flowers with greenish-yellow bases and cross bands of yellow, orange or brown. Very common. 4–10 inches tall. Found in **Brush, Conif.**
First found_____Where_____

67. Pink Fawn Lily, *Erythronium revolutum,* which we have found on Redwood Creek near Willow Creek (Hwy. 299), and in the Siskiyous on the way to Grants Pass, is rather rare, but surely lovely. The 1–4 buds may start out creamy white, with yellow at the base, but soon turn rose-pink in color. Also called Coast Fawn Lily. 4–12 inches tall. Found in **Meadow, Water, Conif.; Str. Wd.**
First found_____Where_____

Oregon Fawn Lily, *Erythronium oregonum* ssp. *leucandrum,* is similar to the above flowers, but the white or pink flowers have reddish or brown bases outside, and yellow within, and their tips are twisted. The flower stems are brownish and about 6 to 12 inches tall. Found in **Conif.**
First found_____Where_____

Notes_____

54. Pitkin Lily
Lilium pitkinense

55. Mission Bells
Fritillaria lanceolata

57. Purdy's Fritillary
Fritillaria purdyi

56. Mendocino Mission Bells
Fritillaria rodericki

58. Scarlet Fritillary
Fritillaria recurva

59. Adobe Lily
Fritillaria pluriflora

60. Hairy Cat's Ear
Calochortus tolmiei

61. Baby Tulip
Calochortus uniflorus

62. Diogenes Lantern
Calochortus amabilis

68. Bear Grass, *Xerophyllum tenax,* also known as Elk Grass, Fire Lily, Pine Lily, or Squaw Grass, is truly spectacular in beauty as well as in historical lore. The wiry tufts of stiff grass from which the tall shafts of blooms arise are grayish-green and very strong. Therefore, they were used by the Indians in the making of baskets and rope, also for the same things by the early pioneers who were glad to find these plants growing by their cabins. They are often seen in mountain meadows and frequently grow on banks along Highway 1. The numerous white flowers appear in a dense, terminal raceme, 4–24 inches long. 1–6 feet tall. Found in **Grass; Conif.**
First found_____Where_____

69. Wake Robin, *Trillium ovatum.* Since the Wake Robins have already done their duty and the Zygadene Lilies are almost a foot high right now in Grandpa Charley's Park, let's take a moment to tell how these and other lovely wildflowers *may* get under your skin, too. For the first year or two we were in this gorgeous natural spot near Gualala, Chas would calmly report new findings rather prosaically, but one sunny morning in early January he called, "Hurry out! Trillies are poking through, and zyggies are up all over the place!"
   Our Wake Robin, or Coast Trillium, has its own little stem which holds the flower way up above the three large leaves; white flowers turn rose color. 8–20 inches tall. Found in **Conif.**
First found_____Where_____

70. Red Trillium or **Giant Wake Robin,** *Trillium chloropetalum,* has its red (also white, see below) blossoms nestling right among the three large leaves, and, therefore is sessile, or without the little stem. 12–20 inches tall. Found in **Conif.; Oak; Str. Wd.; Brush.**
First found_____Where_____

71. White trillium, *Trillium chloropetalum.* Same species as above, but shown in picture is the white variety. Both grow in the damp woods, flowering from early February and on, throughout most of the Redwood Empire. 12–20 inches. Found in **Conif., Oak; Str. Wd.; Brush.**
First found_____Where_____

72. Creek Trillium, *Trillium rivale,* is rather rare and unusual, but may be found along streams with rocky, canyon-like walls. The smaller leaves and longer flower stem give it a more vine-like appearance than its bigger cousins. White petals may be marked with rose-red. 4–11 inches tall. Found

in **Str. Wd.; Rocks; Conif.**
First found_____Where_____

73. Zygadene Lily or **Star Lily,** *Zygadenus fremontii,* is among a genus that has more or less poisonous bulbs. The yellowish-white flowers of this species have clawed petals and appear in rather loose panicles or racemes. The 8–24 inch basal leaves are folded and arched. Found in **Grass; Brush; Conif.**
First found_____Where_____

Death Camas, *Zygadenus venenosus,* is noted for its very poisonous bulb, which has a dark outer coat. The basal leaves are 6–12 inches long and folded, but not arched. The white flowers have both sepals and petals long-clawed. 10–24 inches tall. Found in **Grass; Brush; Conif.; Meadow; Str. Wd.**
First found_____Where_____

Small-Flowered Zygadene, *Zygadenus micranthus,* has flowers only about ¼" long. 8–20 inch tall plant. Raceme. Found in **Brush, Conif.**
First found_____Where_____

Large-Panicled Zygadene, *Zygadenus fontanus.* The large panicles have widely-spreading, horizontal branches; basal leaves folded and rough to touch. 1–3 feet tall. Found in **Conif.; Brush.**
First found_____Where_____

74. Corn Lily, *Veratrum fimbriatum,* is also called False Hellebore. Very stout with long leaves that hug the stock like corn. Grows in great colonies in our Mendocino woodland areas in light or deep shade or even sun. It is a late summer bloomer with blossoms still lovely well into winter. 3–7 foot tall. Found in **Conif.; Meadow.**
First found_____Where_____

75/76. Red Clintonia, *Clintonia andrewsiana,* is a favorite lily of the damp woodsy mixed redwood forest. The very long flower stem has a rosette of large, shiny, bright green leaves clustered at its feet; the reddish flowers form an umbel, which crowns the tall, sturdy stem. Sometimes smaller clusters are found below the main one. The berries are bright blue "jewels." Plant 1–2 feet tall. Found in **Conif.**
First found_____Where_____

Notes_____

63. White Fairy Lantern
Calochortus albus

64. Butterfly Mariposa Lily
Calochortus venustus

65. Slink Pod
Scoliopus bigelovii

66. Cream Fawn Lily
Erythronium californicum

67. Pink Fawn Lily
Erythronium revolutum

68. Bear Grass
Xerophyllum tenax

69. Wake Robin
Trillium ovatum

70. Red Trillium
Trillium chloropetalum

71. White Trillium
Trillium chloropetalum

77. False Solomon's Seal, *Smilacina racemosa,* is often found with Fairy Bells (see below) waving its plumes or bells along some shady bank. This species has numerous white flowers on a large, 1½–7 inch long panicle; the broad, but sharp-pointed leaves clasp the stem near the base. 1–3 feet tall, with mostly red or purple-spotted berries. Found in **Conif.; Str. Wd.**
First found_____Where_____

Nuttall's Solomon Seal, *Smilacina stellata* var. *sessilifolia,* has a few or several white flowers in a short raceme; leaves with 3 prominent veins; berries red. 1–2 feet high. Found in **Conif.; Brush; Str. Wd.**
First found_____Where_____

78. Fairy Bells, *Disporum smithii,* certainly deserves its name, as the delicate pale greenish-white flowers are hidden under the large, oval but sharp-pointed leaves exactly as one might suspect a fairy would do with her bells, which the flowers indeed look like. This species has unusually large flowers, 5/8–1 inch long, so is sometimes called Large-Flowered Fairy Bells, and has light-orange to red berries, looking like delicate jewels. 1–3 feet tall. Found in **Conif.; Str. Wd.**
First found_____Where_____

Hooker's Fairy Bell, *Disporum hookeri,* has a cluster of 1–3 top-shaped flowers, creamy-white to greenish-white in color, turning into bright scarlet berries. 1–2½ feet high. Found in **Conif.; Str. Wd.**
First found_____Where_____

✍ Loasa Family—Loasaceae ✍

79. Blazing Star, *Mentzelia laevicaulis,* often grows on gravel bars on dry creeks, where the stars make a golden glow mornings and evenings. Be careful of the branches; they will stick to your clothes. A flower of the hot summer. The leaves become brittle and rough to the feel; the unusually large, 2–3 inch long, light yellow flowers form clusters of 1–3 at the top of the shining white stem. Plant 1–5 feet tall. Found in **Grass; Brush; Str. Wd.; Oak; Conif.; Hardwd.**
First found_____Where_____

✍ Mallow Family—Malvaceae ✍

80. Wild Hollyhock or **Checkerbloom,** *Sidalcea malvaeflora,* is one of the taller,

bushier mallows, which is found late in the season flowering along our country roads. Its lower stem is covered with coarse hairs; the broad, well-rounded leaves are 3/4–2 inches wide and rather fleshy as well as hairy, each on a long stem, and with 7–9 lobes; the usually simple racemes are dense to open, with rose-pink to rarely white flowers, usually white-veined on the petals, which are short-beaked. 6–18 inches tall. Found in **Grass; Brush.**
First found_____Where_____ _____

Fringed Sidalcea, *Sidalcea diploscypha,* is one of the common pink to purple mallows of the coast, but the pink petals often have a deep purplish spot. It is a simple or few branched plant, with conspicuous finger-like bracts, often with still finer divisions or filaments surrounding the flowers. The plant is covered with fine hairs. 8–18 inches tall. Found in **Grass; Brush.**
First found_____Where_____

～ Meadow Foam Family—Limnanthaceae ～

81. Meadow Foam, *Limnanthes douglasii,* covers our mountain meadows with its soft and glowing yellow-white haze, charming both close by and in the distance, surely an early April delight. It is a widely-varied plant, with some petals all yellow, some white, and others yellow with white tips, each bowl-shaped and with a U-shaped band of short hairs at base of each petal. 4–16 inches tall. Found in **Meadow; Grass; Water.**
First found_____Where_____

～ Milkwort Family—Polygalaceae ～

California Milkwort, *Polygala californica,* is abundant in openings and pastures in the Mendocino coast area. Here in Grandpa Charley's Park the foliage is branchy and low-growing, bronzy purple. The blossoms, very like little sweetpeas, are rosy or pale rose, and appear in distinctly short-stemmed racemes, each with 3–10 loose flowers. Leaves have sharp, stiff hairs along veins. 1–14 inches tall. Found in **Grass; Brush.**
First found_____Where_____

Notes_____

72. Creek Trillium
Trillium rivale

73. Zygadene Lily
Zygadenus fremontii

74. Corn Lily
Veratrum fimbriatum

75. Red Clintonia Fruit
Clintonia andrewsiana

76. Red Clintonia
Clintonia andrewsiana

77. False Solomon's Seal
Smilacina racemosa

79. Blazing Star
Mentzelia laevicaulis

78. Fairy Bells
Disporum smithii

81. Meadow Foam
Limnanthes douglasii

80. Wild Hollyhock
Sidalcea malvaeflora

✦ Morning-Glory Family—Convolvulaceae ✦

82. Beach Morning-Glory, *Convolvulus soldanella,* finds sandy beaches ideal for its spreading habits, since it spreads flatly over the sand to avoid the wind. The stems are fleshy; the shining leaves are almost as broad as long; the rose to purple flowers appear like short funnels, 1½–2 inches long. It stretches out for 4 to 20 inches across the sand. Found at **Beach.**
First found_____Where_____

Common Bindweed, *Convolvulus arvensis,* is a pest of our orchards and fields, twining or creeping over the ground, with single stems holding up the white to pinkish flowers, each about ½ to 2 inches wide at mouth. Plant 1–3 feet long. Found in **Grass; Cultiv.**
First found_____Where_____

✦ Mustard Family—Cruciferae ✦

Spring Beauty, *Dentaria californica,* also called Toothwort or Milkmaids, often flowers in February. Colors range from white to very bright rose-purple. It is probably our best known very early flower, a cheerful welcome to spring, and surely a beauty. 4–16 inches tall. Found in **Str. Wd.; Conif.; Oak; Brush; Grass.**
First found_____Where_____

✦ Orchid Family—Orchidaceae ✦

83 & 84. Redwood Orchid, *Calypso bulbosa,* answers also to Fairyslipper, Angel's Slipper, and Deer-head Orchid. It is one of our earliest spring flowers, and near sea-level, a single bloom or two may be found in the first of February, so there is a long season for finding these rose-pink beauties bursting into glorious color in the mountain glades. These dainty plants show their appreciation of the first warm September rains by unfurling a single leaf out into a point to support the forthcoming bud-capped stem. Entire mossy logs may be covered by a colony of calypsos. A new weighing-in-station for a local lumber mill was about to doom a small log section covered by moss and calypsos, sturdy in spite of nearby tossed beer cans, when we rescued the flowers. Careless picking and logging destroys these beauties, but it can be stopped. Squirrels eat the bulbs. 2–10 inches tall. Found in **Conif.; Str. Wd.**
First found_____Where_____

California Ladyslipper, *Cypripedium californicum,* clusters in shaded woods or banks of moist limestone; beautiful and rare, but once seen, never to be forgotten. This species has alternate leaves and 5/8 inch long green yellow sepals. Petal lip white or pinkish. 1–2 feet tall. Found in **Conif.; Rocks.**
First found_____Where_____

85. Clustered Ladyslipper, *Cypripedium fasciculatum,* is smaller (2–6 inches tall), has opposite leaves, and a greenish-yellow lip to the flower. Found in **Conif.; Rocks.**
First found_____Where_____

86. Chatterbox Orchid, *Epipactis gigantea,* or Stream Orchid, is a stoutish plant, which lives along wet stream banks. The rosy blossoms are typically orchid-like, but unlike the rarer orchids, they may be found in great colonies in summer. Flowers in racemes. 1–3 feet tall. Found in **Conif.; Oak; Str. Wd.; Brush.**
First found_____Where_____

87 & 88. Phantom Orchid, *Eburophyton austinae* (from the Latin words meaning Ivory Plant because it is not green; often called Ghost Plant). It has a single white stem 8–10 inches or more tall with waxy-white, golden-throated flowers in a terminal raceme. Like the calypsos, phantom orchids are often found in colonies, but are actually quite rare. We came across our first one unexpectedly in early June, 1958, as we were helping prepare our sister's Orleans ranch for summer visitors. Grandson Mike came running in from the forest with the exciting announcement that Grandpa Charley had found a snow plant! It was a snow-white plant, all right. Three tall single stems rose from the edge of a rotten log, ending in waxy-white and plump, sort of globe-shaped flowers. Inside we could see the shining, golden spot on the throat, while from the plant rose a heavenly fragrance. As Grandpa likes to tease, we forgave him for calling it a Snow Plant. Since then we have had the pleasure of finding phantoms in other places near Orleans, in several shady, deeply forested glades in southern Mendocino County, and inland towards Mt. Anthony. We hope the thrill of *your* first phantom orchid will be as lasting as ours, but please save the flower and teach others not to pick these rare beauties. Found in **Conif.**
First found_____Where_____

Notes_____

82. Beach Morning-Glory
Convolvulus soldanella

85. Clustered Ladyslipper
Cypripedium fasciculatum

83. Redwood Orchid
Calypso bulbosa

84. Albino Calypso
Calypso bulbosa

86. Chatterbox Orchid
Epipactus gigantea

88. Phantom Orchid
Eburophyton austinae

87. Phantom Orchid
Eburophyton austinae

89. Coral Root
Corallorhiza maculata

89. Coral Root, *Corallorhiza maculata,* or Spotted Coral Root, is the spotted species. All Coral Roots stand stiffly at attention as you pass through their deeply shaded forest home. They stay in bloom a long time; the blossoms are succeeded by equally interesting seed pods, which hang down from the stems like ornaments. 8–20 inches tall. Found in **Conif.**
First found_____Where_____

Striped Coral Root, *Corallorhiza striata,* has the flower longitudinally striped. 6–20 inches tall. Found in **Conif.**
First found_____Where_____

🖝 Oxalis Family—Oxalidaceae 🖝

90. Redwood Sorrel, *Oxalis oregana,* is truly a "sour" grass which carpets our redwood forests everywhere with its clover-like foliage. We transplanted some mangled plants from a logging road and they did very well until two of our frequent young fawn visitors decided to see if they *were* good to eat. Apparently the deer were only curious since other patches in the woods are seldom disturbed by them. The pink bloom glows brightly in the rounded clusters of shamrock-like leaves. 3–8 inches tall. Found in **Conif.**
First found_____Where_____

🖝 Pea Family—Leguminosae 🖝

91. Redbud, *Cercis occidentalis,* is among many members of the Pea Family that contribute a great deal to our spring and summer parade of color. Lake County is famous for its Redbud flowers, but the plant is scattered throughout the Redwood Empire, and ranges from shrubs to branchy trees, entirely clothed in springtime in sparkling, rosy magenta blossoms before the leaves unfold. 6–20 feet tall. Found in **Oak; Brush.**
First found_____Where_____

92. Chaparral Pea. *Pickeringia montana,* is equally bright, but its blossoms are often hidden by the pale green foliage and appear later in the summer. Watch out for its spines! Branches very stiff; leaves tiny, palmately 1–3; the large rosy flowers are solitary. 2–7 feet tall. Found in **Brush.**
First found_____Where_____

93. Large-Flowered Lotus or **Persian Carpet,** *Lotus grandiflorus,* does look like such a carpet when seen in its favorite haunt, a sunny, mountain

meadow, with its many different color combinations, orange, through gold, yellow, and cream. Its purple with splashes of red dots and stripes has to be seen to be appreciated. Imagine all this done in velvet trailers on the ground or climbing through taller grasses and you have found Lotus. It is covered with sharp and stiff, incurved and pressed down hairs. 7–9 leaflets; 2 or more yellow to red flowers in umbels. 8–24 inches long. Found in **Conif.; Oak; Brush; Str. Wd.; Grass.**
First found_____Where_____

∾ Pink Family—Caryophyllaceae ∾

Many of our choicest pinks are pink in color, true indeed, but they are called pinks because their blossoms seems to have been cut from sparkling cloth with pinking shears.

94. Indian Pink, *Silene californica,* makes a brilliant splash of "Indian crimson" against the greenery and rocks of our clayey roadside banks. Sticky to touch. 6–15 inches tall. Found in **Brush; Oak; Conif.**
First found_____Where_____

95. Fringed Pink, *Silene hookeri,* is found mainly from Humboldt Co. north, but we have seen it near Willits in Mendocino Co. It is simply exquisite, shining away among the withered oak leaves high on a dry, rocky bank. The pink foliage is hairy, grayish, and usually spreads from a central, very deep root system prostrate on the ground; the grayish leaves often finger-like. The petals are white to pink or violet, the seeds purplish-black. 2–6 inches long. Found in **Conif.; Rocks.**
First found_____Where_____

∾ Pitcher-Plant Family—Sarraceniaceae ∾

96. Cobra Lily, *Darlingtonia californica,* a bog and creekside plant with leaves modified into tubes down which unwary insects crawl to check out "gastric" liquid in the bowl-like bottom where they die. Also, Darlingtonia is the title of the newsletter of the Northcoast Chapter of the California Native Plant Society. Found in **Marsh; Str. Wd.**
First found_____Where_____

Notes_____

91. Redbud
Cercis occidentalis

90. Redwood Sorrel
Oxalis oregana

92. Chaparral Pea
Pickeringia montana

94. Indian Pink
Silene californica

93. Lotus
Lotus grandiflorus

95. Fringed Pink
Silene hookeri

96. Cobra Lily
Darlingtonia californica

☙ Pond Lily Family—Nymphaeaceae ❧

97. Yellow Pond Lily, or **Water Lily,** *Nymphaea polysepala,* lives in ponds and lakes. The seeds were a common food for the Indians in the old days. Leaves either float or are erect and are deeply heart-shaped; flowers large and yellow to purplish. Plant 4 to 6 feet long. Found in **Water.**
First found_____Where_____

☙ Primrose Family—Primulaceae ❧

98. Star Flower, *Trientalis latifolia,* is a slender plant with beautifully shaped pale pink stars on delicate stems above large, fan-shaped leaves. It gives the impression of fairy-like grace beneath the towering giants of the redwood forest. 2–8 inches tall. Found in **Conif.**
First found_____Where_____

99 & 100. Henderson's Shooting Star, *Dodecatheon hendersonii,* whose brilliant magenta-purple blooms are accented by a black point in the center, are sometimes called bird-bills. Among our very earliest spring blossoms, they are also among the showiest and are to be found in clusters along roadsides protected by low brush. The petals are abruptly bent downward and backward. 3–12 inches tall. Found in **Oak; Brush; Str. Wd.; Grass.**
First found_____Where_____

101. To find **Blue** or **Scarlet Pimpernel,** *Anagallis arvensis,* separately is an enjoyable experience, but imagine finding them growing side by side! Although a weed, the blossoms, with their flat and slightly attached petals (sometimes white too) are very attractive. 4–10 inches tall. Found in **Cultiv.; Grass; Brush.**
First found_____Where_____

☙ Purslane or Portulaca Family—Portulacaceae ❧

102. Red Maids, *Calandrinia ciliata,* have succulent, wide-spreading stems, which support the many rose blooms of this common roadside and meadow beauty. The racemes of 3–7, soft, rose-red flowers are lovely. 2–8 inches tall. Found in **Cultiv.; Grass.**
First found_____Where_____

103. Cliff Maidens, *Lewisia cotyledon,* is one of our very favorite wildflowers. It grows high up on rocky cliffs from a deep tap root, topped with a cluster of thick leaves from which grow slender stems each capped with a luscious many-petaled, whitish, waxy bloom. The exquisite gleaming daintiness of the plant is further accented by the fact that the mid-rib of each petal is a pure streak of bright magenta or rosy pink. One entire rocky bank of these fascinating flowers was blasted away on Hwy. 96 at Bluff Creek to provide a safer road into the Klamath River area. Summer bloomers these are, and they are worth looking for. 4–12 inches tall. Found in **Rocks.**
First found_____Where_____

🌿 Rose Family—Rosaceae 🌿

Wild roses are numerous, but the entire Rose Family has many seemingly unrelated members.

104. Wild Rose or **Wood Rose,** *Rosa gymnocarpa,* is probably the most common of the genus. The large flowers (with ½ inch petals) are usually solitary and red in color; the branches are lined with slender, straight prickles. 3–10 feet. Found in **Oak; Brush; Conif.; Str. Wd.**
First found_____Where_____

105. Sea Foam, Ocean Spray or **Cream Bush,** *Holodiscus discolor,* has dark red to brownish or gray older bark, which shreds with age; twigs straw-colored. The tiny creamy white flowers are so numerous they well deserve the beautiful name of spray; leaves deeply-toothed. 4–20 feet. Found in **Conif.; Brush.**
First found_____Where_____

106. Salmonberry, *Rubus spectabilis,* produces beautiful red to yellow to salmon-colored berries in the summer that look very much like salmon eggs. The older twigs and branches have yellowish, shredding bark; leaves with 3 leaflets, each double-toothed; the scattered red-purple flowers appear in groups of 1–4. 6–13 feet tall. Found in **Conif.**
First found_____Where_____

Notes_____

97. Yellow Pond Lily
Nymphaea polysepala

98. Star Flower
Trientalis latifolia

99. Shooting Star
Dodecatheon hendersonii

100. Shooting Stars
Dodecatheon hendersonii

101. Scarlet Pimpernel
Anagallis arvensis

103. Cliff Maidens
Lewisia cotyledon

102. Redmaids
Calandrinia ciliata

104. Wild Rose
Rosa gymnocarpa

ᴖ Silk-Tassel Family—Garryaceae ᴖ

107. Coast Silk-Tassel Bush, *Garrya elliptica,* hangs out its jeweled catkins ever so much like strings of beads very early in the spring, in January even, on the coast. The highly-polished leather leaves give the bush a glorious sheen, which enhances the swinging jewels. The hairs of the lower leaf surface in this species are usually curly or wavy; leaves quite broad. Up to 25 feet tall. Found in **Brush; Conif.; Sea Bluffs.**
First found_____Where_____

Fremont's Silk-Tassel, *Garrya fremontii,* is smaller, 5–15 feet tall, with the lower leaf surface mostly smooth. Found in **Brush; Conif.**
First found_____Where_____

ᴖ Saxifrage Family—Saxifragaceae ᴖ

108. Wild Currant or **Red Flowering Currant,** *Ribes glutinosum,* is a bush with brownish to gray old bark; leaves round and kidney shaped, dark green above, whitish below; the deep rose flowers have narrow tubes, the petals sometimes pale red; berries black, with a bloom. 3–12 feet. Found in **Conif.; Str. Wd.**
First found_____Where_____

109. Canyon Gooseberry, *Ribes menziesii.* Probably the commonest gooseberry in the area. Young twigs are densely bristly. Older branches have 3 spines at nodes. The fruit is clothed with bristles; flowers red-purplish, usually very profuse. Plant about 40 inches high. Found in **Rocks; Str. Wd.**
First found_____Where_____

ᴖ Stonecrop Family—Crassulaceae ᴖ

110. Yellow Stonecrop, *Sedum spathulifolium,* has shining yellow, almost star-like blooms held up on tall, thick stems. Sturdy is the word for stonecrops, since they live on rocks both in the mountains and along the sea where winds drag at them. Petals rarely orange or white. 2–12 inches. Found in **Rocks.**
First found_____Where_____

111. Hens-And-Chickens or **Sea Lettuce,** *Dudleya farinosa,* glistens handsomely against the weathered rocks above the sea. The little rosettes, each

with 14–30 leaves, all densely white-mealy to green; flower stems also white-mealy; flowers pale yellow, sometimes red-flecked. 2–6 inches. Found in **Sea Bluffs.**
First found_____Where_____

✺ Sunflower Family—Compositae ✺

Common California Aster, Aster chilensis, is a member of the largest of all the plant families. But because we are concentrating on jewel flowers of outstanding interest, we give only one example here. This species shines its lavender and yellow and white flowers in tall ranks along our highways, and even glows brightly through the dust of less frequented country lanes. The flowers extend away from each other by degrees in an open panicle, each flower with 20–35 rays, each ¼–½ inch long. Plant 16–40 inches tall. Found in **Grass; Meadow; Cultiv.; Brush; Oak; Str. Wd.; Conif.**
First found_____Where_____

✺ Sweet-Shrub Family—Calycanthaceae ✺

Spice Bush or Sweet-Shrub, Calycanthus occidentalis, will surprise you one day as you travel through a mountain canyon, lightly shaded and moist. The unusual blossoms are cinnamon-red in color; the leaves are spicy and aromatic when bruised. 3–19 feet tall. Found in **Str. Wd.**
First found_____Where_____

✺ Violet Family—Violaceae ✺

Redwood Violet, Viola sempervirens, is a constant bloomer here in the warm area known as the banana belt on the southern Mendocino Coast. The creeping plants make a carpet, yellow-starred, in company with calypsos, vancouveria, redwood oxalis, and ginger. They are so gentle, small, and demure that the ferns which hover about seem gigantic. The lemon-yellow petals may be faintly purple-veined. Stems lie along ground; 4–12 inches long. Found in **Conif.**
First found_____Where_____

✺ Waterleaf Family—Hydrophyllaceae ✺

Baby Blue-Eyes, Nemophila menziesii, is one of our sweetest summer sky-blue gems. It will be found clinging to moist banks, or on protected streams.

105. Sea Foam
Holodiscus discolor

108. Wild Currant
Ribes glutinosum

106. Salmonberry
Rubus spectabilis

107. Coast Silk-Tassel Bush
Garrya elliptica

109. Gooseberry
Ribes menziesii

110. Yellow Stonecrop
Sedum spathulifolium

111. Live-Forever
Dudleya farinosa

112. False Pink Asparagus
Hemitomes congestum

113. Sugarstick
Allotropa virgata

As its family name indicates, it is a tender plant, but it gladly shares its luminous beauty if treated gently. 4–12 inches tall. Found in **Grass; Meadow; Brush; Conif.; Oak.**
First found_____Where_____

Small-Flowered Nemophila, Nemophila parviflora, is another small, tender plant, but with whitish blooms. Found in **Conif.; Oak.**
First found_____Where_____

✌ Wintergreen or Pyrola Family—Pyrolaceae ✌

112. False Pink Asparagus, Hemitomes (Newberrya) congestum, is saprophytic, since it lives on lifeless plant matter in deep, densely shaded forests. It pushes through the forest floor in masses, each individual flower appearing exactly like an asparagus point coming through the ground. Often the points are roundish, like pink wax lily bulbs, or sometimes rosy red. It is a true treasure. 1–6 inches tall. Found in **Conif.**
First found_____Where_____

113 & 114. Sugarsticks, Allotropa virgata, are also saprophytic, since they spring up from deep forest duff, in glorious, glistening red and white, looking like Christmas candy canes, and with green coloring entirely lacking. They are shown here in two growth stages, but there are other stages also, and the plants are very long-lived. Beautiful and rare (because of the foolish people who pick them without thought of beauty's destruction), it is pleasant to find them even in the fall when they stand in dried splendor, each jewel-like blossom in miniature perfection. We have seen colonies of 22 with 2 or 3 of the sticks over 2 foot tall. 4–24 inches. Found in **Conif.**
First found_____Where_____

115. Leafless pyrola, Pyrola aphylla, is a glowing gem to find in the deep forest. Either alone or in groups, the waxy blooms with red-purple sepals and pink to greenish petals with white margins, swing up the thick, usually reddish stem like rosy apple blossoms. The style turns downward in the center of each bloom. Exploring at different elevations, we find the early blooming season at lower levels, but it is a thrill to find the same pyrola species in much brighter colors higher up. 4–8 inches tall. Found in **Conif.**
First found_____Where_____

Large Wintergreen, *Pyrola bracteata,* has rose-purple or dull red flowers, and large basal leaves. 8–16 inches. Found in **Conif.**
First found_____Where_____

116. Prince's Pine or **Pipsissewa,** *Chimaphila menziesii,* is truly winter-loving, or wintergreen, and is a delicately-fashioned, low-growing plant, with leather-like and shining leaves. The perfectly-shaped blossoms appear as if made of plastic. Showy white or pink blossoms may greet you along a deep forest trail. Leaves ovate. Plant 3–5 inches tall. Found in **Conif.; Brush; Hardwd.**
First found_____Where_____

Little Prince's Pine, *Chimaphila umbellata* var. *occidentalis,* has pink blossoms and more slender, oblanceolate leaves. It is found on drier, higher ground. 6–12 inches. Found in **Conif.; Brush.**
First found_____Where_____

117. Indian Pipe, *Monotropa uniflora* (often called Ghost Pipe). Rare, waxy-white saprophyte; turns black. Found in **Conif.; Brush.**
First found_____Where_____

118. White Groundcone or **Lala,** *Pleuricospora fimbriolata.* The common name was coined by Charles Young to convey their striking appearance. Flowers appear at first white, later yellow, or turning dark brown, occurs only in deep humus of dense forests. Found in **Conif.**
First found_____Where_____

119. Snowplant, *Sarcodes sanguinea.* Stems solitary or in clusters. Grows only in deep humus. Found in **Conif.**
First found_____Where_____

120. Pityopus, *Pityopus californicus.* Name originates from the Greek, *pitus,* pine, and *pus,* foot, because of where it lives. It is a rare plant and requires the deep, dark humus of the old-growth forest. Found in **Conif.**
First found_____Where_____

Notes_____

_____

_____

_____

114. Sugarsticks
Allotropa virgata

117. Indian Pipe
Monotropa uniflora

115. Leafless pyrola
Pyrola aphylla

116. Prince's Pine
Chimaphila menziesii

118. White Groundcone
Pleuricospora fimbriolata

119. Snowplant
Sarcodes sanguinea

120. Pityopus
Pityopus californicus

Index By Photo Number